Stories About Wooden Keyboards

Kendrick Smithyman

STORIES ABOUT
WOODEN KEYBOARDS

Auckland University Press
Oxford University Press

First published 1985

Published with the assistance of the
New Zealand Literary Fund

Printed in New Zealand
by University of Auckland Printing Services
from type set by Typocrafters Ltd
ISBN 0 19 648049 3

IN MEMORIAM
Christopher
1947–1984

ACKNOWLEDGEMENTS

Acknowledgements are made to those publications where some of these poems have previously appeared: *Craccum, Islands, Landfall, Kiwi, Still Life after Kafka, Span, Northern Light* (Canada), *Humanities Review* (India), *Poetry New Zealand* and *The Oxford Book of Contemporary New Zealand Poetry.*

'Levertov's Hypocrite Women' relates to Denise Levertov's 'Hypocrite Women' from earlier in her career, and 'Sylvia' to Section II of her *Candles in Babylon* (1982), the section called 'Pig Dreams'.

'395' draws on No. 395 of Ossip Mandestam's *Collected Works* in the version of Clarence Brown and W. S. Merwin, *Ossip Mandelstam: Selected Poems* (1973).

'After Ondra Lysohorsky' was sparked off by Ewald Oser's translation of Lysohorsky's 'Lachia' which appeared in *The London Magazine* in 1972.

'Pasternak: Theme with Variations' and 'Pasternak: The Making of a Poet' make use especially of the prose *Safe Conduct* (trans. A. Brown, 1959) and poems of *Fifty Poems* (trans. Lydia Pasternak Slater, 1963).

'Fin de la Belle Époque: Misia's View' and 'Death in Venice: Diaghilev' are adapted from Arthur Gold and Robert Fizdale, *Misia: the Life of Misia Sert* (1980), especially pp. 163–4 and pp. 260–1. Of the dramatic incidents attending Diaghilev's death it should be said that Gold and Fizdale do not altogether agree with Serge Lifar (1965; English version 1970, p. 74) or with Lifar (1948). Richard Buckle, *Diaghilev* (1979, p. 541) also differs.

'Peehi/Best' is indebted to the biography of Elsdon Best by the late Elsdon Craig; 'Baucke' to the entry in the *D.N.Z.B.* and to *Where the White Man Treads*; 'Rinaua/Lindauer' to ed. J. C. Graham, *Maori Paintings by Gottfried Lindauer*; for 'Pomare' and 'Te Rangi Hiroa/Buck', see Buck's *Vikings of the Sunrise* (1938, p. 162) and *The Coming of the Maori* (1949, p. 410).

CONTENTS

DREAMS, RESPONSIBILITIES

In that dream Mozart is always
on the road to Prague, beating it out.
Meanwhile seethe foul woods straight from
Salvator Rosa, with banditti
biting their nails. He won't make it.

Or Wagner, stormtost in the Baltic?
Easy to believe they were not sirens
howled the shrouds under, deep by deep.
Where met the Dutchman, yet to be met?
And Elsa, her breasts lifting like
serpents at their nests . . . dread the rest.

Alessandro Marcello perhaps.
He goes to a masked ball, that's what
you'd like to think for him, stepping
from a gondola—almost you hear
retiring his boatman's song—he enters
some colonnade's obscurity. Then
the knife presented, the demand!

Try to practise at an art in conscience
(this your Unconscious informs)
at risk. You must learn to live dangered.
You give offence. You do not see faces
clearly. You're preyed upon, accused.
Here I stand, I cannot other.

WITH NO [   ]

With no [   ] subject → noun
I confront my typewriter
to which I am subject. → verb of noun

Respect objects. They have
their own lives to live
for us. They tend our reasons.

Like the creatures of dreams,   → actor
those activities of dream which   → action
justify themselves. It was a dream

I spoke about. You attempted
this, you did that. Everywhere
a winter blew disenchanting.

You showed me what you'd done.
I asked in that minute desert
where frostnipped brussel sprouts
wavered in some prodigal clarity,

"Yes, I like it. But why did you need
to buy an abandoned brickworks?"
A sense of liberty? How it is elusive.

In dreams one may feel free, to fly.   → chg to impersonal
Winter airs scarified their fields.   pronoun
So much talk. I telephoned,
                        personal, specific

Saying importantly, "Are you there?
Oh good, you are there." Before long
I shall write another letter.

LEVERTOV'S HYPOCRITE WOMEN

If at Mills College sweetly a rain shifted
from branch to branch, tree to tree,
trees themselves heady of womenly women
who, having blossomed, bloom again
auditors of mists, fruits, flowers and a gusty
throaty bellowing sacramental bull poet
whose air, whose day, eternally trend westward,
oceanward, if then

like so many forms of Europa
(as you read it)
the visiting poet charges them: their privacies are
noisome, wrinkled, hairy, to the Moon
subservient, caves of the Hag, ugly—
how they simmer and hum, to agree.
Ah this (they whisper) we have thought too.
We're not ashamed. "They are not for the eye."

Heh, get the superiority of the streaming bull
stamping his ground in a Mills Valley grove,
his trees bent down to fruitful women,
their heads bent down, obedient.

What in Mills College it is to walk a poet!
So muscular, vaticinating, not
to lumber away indoors, away from the rain. To hold
his liberated audience, washing their shame
if not their stain from them.
After, they all strolled down to Jordan,
and crossed over? Waving strands of almond,
cried upon Semele? As far as Santa Barbara?

Dubitable authority, who hasn't stood
out in delicate rainfall, bemused,
charged to disagree, memorising
one not such cave, celebrating.
Not to apologise.
We want an aesthetic which does not keep its distance.
Neither noisome nor wrinkled, unpredictably
cyclamen neat, handsomely sculpted
but no sculpting was its like,
or her service, sacramental.

STORIES ABOUT WOODEN KEYBOARDS

That notable Pole, their pianist,
supremely their patriot, their first President
his countrymen's darling, darling of
highest society's *belle époque,*
he travelled the world with a wooden keyboard,
his practised toy. In an Atlantic liner's suite,
a stateroom on the Union Pacific,
at hotel windows commanding some boulevard
stippled with Monegasque vowels like flower baskets,
hour after hour he sat, his hands working,
working. After he went out—to Wigmore Hall,
Salle Pleyel, Carnegie, the Opera House.
There he put his hands to work. Acclaimed,
he made them legends. Everyone heard them,
knew them by heart. The heart was his, in them.
He stepped into his carriage and drew away.

Where pick up a story about a man in prison,
more likely a prisoner of war camp?
He got hold of a slab of wood,
something as ordinary as a bit of six by one, say.
Scratched on it with (suppose) a nail.
He etched a keyboard.

A notable Pole, he stopped being President.
He travelled the world on like Atlantic liners,
growing older. When asked would he play
he might agree, only if salon lights were turned down
so nobody saw his fingers arthritic knots,
the mistakes they were making.
Everyone pretended. He still had red hair?

That man in the *Stalag,* I know about him.
He played upon silence. That was what he had.
In the inner ear, by heart he got, a soprano
musicking *Hate! I loathe you. You're driving
me out of my mind . . . you want to commit me.*
He sweated it out at his keyboard. Silence was
just about all he had to play on. He didn't have
                    to like it.

People who shared the hut with him pretended
not to hear. He sat for hours working his hands.
He might look through the mesh window,
through the camp's perimeter wire. Sometimes
in fields beyond he saw peasant women.
Perhaps one like you, as far apart.

[handwritten annotations: "what's the diff b'twn a duck?" with arrows marking "1" and "2" pointing to circled words, and "semantic anomaly?"]

SKATEBOARDING WITH LEWIS CARROLL

Comedy of the world, our time's
commodity by which we try
to be amused. It ends delight
supposedly.
        Those children went
before the wind, they sailed over
sleek plane of the reservoir,
they flew. Their sails crowded, drew,
and danced; their skateboards made music
for them who were not birds to wheel
as they wheeled, not dancers, nor were
they dazzling yachts, but briefly seemed.
Then wind died, delight died.
It's time like that to furl your sail,
go home perhaps, step a mirror
through to another side, other-
ly instructed.
        Be reconciled
to being reconciled, to making
do made over. *Drink me, drink me!*
bottles plead. Learn to shrink small,
tidy, docile, dry.
        Along roads
between two main ways orchards are
cutting back lost seasons' growing.
Clump by clump they fire their wasted
woods, smoke like battlefields' spoils
towards the creek.
        Like battlefield
smoke in Roger Fenton's pictures
of the Crimea, as light, almost
stilled, chilling deceit. This fact
concordant, when its fact was gone
past into likeness. At Ripon
Lewis Carroll saw pictures shown
just days before the war itself
was gone, Fenton's pictures. Bells rang
throughout, flags flew all over town.
He'd not yet met with Alice; that, a month
more. 'I mark this day with a white stone.'

Language of delight deceives noone.
We must go undeceived
through/behind our looking glass

14

wheeling, brief dancers in some air
which plays with us, bemused.
Winds die
like wars away from us. Likeness,
rightness (of gesture, say) catches
at your breath. *Drink me,* dear, *drink me*
before I'm tidy, docile, dry.

FOR THE RECORD

Do not put on an
other record. In
stead, listen to the
quiet which succeeds. Right
now, somewhere at hand
are thoughts which were form
erly dear to men,
tenanting shrub and
bush beyond a neut
ral window. Like a
college of old in
struments they play faith
ful to their score, their
text—purpose nothing
more to apprehend
having done with that.
You hear them breathe, in
sympathy. As though
they were leaves moved to
renounce, semblance of
small birds homed to their
tree, one small section's
creatures liberated
into one day's one form
al terminus.
                    Cre
do quiam absurd
um est. And, Indiv
iduum non est
possibile. So
they say, airing fan
cies like melaleuca
or luculia—
not any more, they
insisted. Their voices
are thinking in ways
our creek used to think
before it was soph
isticated, re
gulated, treacher
ously fallible.
Yet so far, keep faith.

Station yourself be
fore the last of the
light covertly steps
behind cedar, cross
es road, goes uphill
to become first sun
set, then concourse of
sodium flares at motor
way junction with a
burden of traffic
which overbears least
thought of quiet. Every
one's going home. Moment
arily you have
heard. Be assured, by
night we shall rise air
ily confident
through our roofs, adroit
as birds or leaves, more
thin than paper we
may be mistaken
for insubstantial
fictions, shall exchange
shapes of words and what
most informs those shapes,
fitting them into
common text. For some
time we may be other
than a record tracking
at the end of its play,
just tracking, tracking.

DECONSTRUCTING

I'm not going to try describing that run
from down by the creek where it starts being
a river, up to the ridge where everything falls
away westward. For the first time again
you look out on a sea bigger, further, than remembered.
Although, you have waited for it
                                        from down there
where *shabby, ramshackle, derelict* are just terms
for occupation. An abandoned railway line's last
station, scruffy general store also garage,
wornout fridges at roadside where used to be
old milkcans for meat and mail; after,
that place where the post office was and the school
then, and then where the school before that was.
It's all sheep now.
                    God, how many years of it
passing through, passing by. I was transported,
have driven, drive. Going from here to there,
that's a text. And another text, and one more, rewritten.
The seeing part, and saying part:

I said to one wife, replied.
I said to another wife, replied.
Each, another text, another saying, another seeing.
Neither did the one see or other say but yet
what one saw another has or has not said,
while I am telling one what I am thinking/said
to other ("Around this bend used to be
a hell of a big pothole—*whang!* Still is")
as if it were always true. We live by
what's past made over 'As if', so many milkcans,
so many projects for the future

You can't step twice into the same river.
What you first dipped toe in was only as if, truly.
But when you get up on the top, and the sea
is there, the remembering of it as well
from before first perhaps, that's another
part of a text and feels like
                              the same again.
Heraclitus was only talking about rivers,
or about when a shallow creek running over stone
begins to think that it's a river.

BACKGROUND MUSIC (I)

Baron Karl von Schönstein wrote it down, years after
one day at Zseliz, Hungary, eighteen twenty-four.
A house party walking, Schubert with them,
schoolteacher, family tutor, Esterhazy's
music master, out with his gentry for an airing.
They returned into a mindful state of eighteen
twenty-four . . . always, commitments.
Things to be done, have to be done.

They crossed the kitchen, homecoming.
Heard, at her duties, a maid by the stove, who sang.
The household musicmaster caught her tune.
So, his Hungarian Melody (D.817).

Like that, caught if not quite like that
naturally. It required to pass through
versions, asked for changes in key
(but always worked back as a minor).
To a rational identity, attained: as a code number.
Codes do not underwrite what is plangent.

Through all change stayed however faithful
to a girl's singing, without need
for words in any language.

GHOST TOWN

Read all about it, news which never
made the front, even the third, page of *Truth*.
Rapine, assault, deceit, massacre, then long
indolent sunbaked or rainswept silences,
driven sand stinging bones,
driven sand moulding hills, shaping them over
again. Passionate custom demands
a harsh midsummer blue light
with flake-white undertones, gets it, time
and again. With fidelity to experience
they lumbered there, burning

not to uncover bones, otherwise searching
each other, lumbering sand at tide reach,
seriocomic progression of two.
Ritually surfcasting rods bent, bowed,
like fishing birds, like trees walking.
You went by them, unacknowledged.
News of them would never have made any headline.

At night, a murderous drumming in the campground
washroom. In the washed out white night quiet after
heard Time count them out. We are drained, bleached,
not to signify. Two days later, crossed
the old frontier.

WHOEVER

Whatever made that range of hills fall over?
Why, it was no more than only one push from
her neat right hand which is believed not bigger
than a child's hand. But to do, thus able.

Whatever took that parched—almost a moonscape!
with no more pressure than a fingertip's
traced where a flow should rise . . . and there it welled
forseeably, inevitably as any art causing
God's plenty if not of roses then of other
exquisite flowering, in due season. Nobody could
imagine why this before was not imagined,
why not attempted, attained; so kissed
each other in benison, in thanksgiving.

Who was it channelled an injudicious flood
or made obedient the tides' insurgence?
Required the caverned worm to sing a chorus;
what was darkness became light, all lyric?
After, naturally, at every fireside knew
any chant of the people, stories of kinship,
would rule on a right mask for proper dances
at their right time, or how to pursue
most cunning shade of meaning out
of most favoured riddles? Yet had
no proper name herself, lived mainly apart?

This afternoon I read of a folk
who have no name, calling themselves simply
The People, find hard to account the ways of others,
lack a term for the World let alone what is worldly.
Sometimes, however, they will exchange seeds
along with myths neither party may grasp.

Almost any man's story.
Caught out in rain sensitive as lovemaking
suddenly he thinks of her, stops where he is
being again all desert. He cannot move.

THE LAST MORIORI

Reputedly last of his kind,
quite surely one of the last
not crossbred but (as They said) pure
as pure goes, a Chatham Island Moriori
taken for a slave when a boy, taken
again in some other raiding, passed
from band to band, from place to place
until he washed up on the River.
That was the story, anyway, which is
as may be. He was

very old, he did not belong,
some chunk of totara which lay too long
        in acid swamp.
He was kumara left on the pit's floor,
        sweetness dried, its hull drawn small.
He was what you found in caves but did not
        mention, travesty gone
beyond human. A tatty topcoat, bowler hat,
blanket which seemed to look your way
without seeing you from the stoop of a hut
at the Pa. A few weak hungers,
he survived. He endured,

already myth, beyond legends of his kind,
a poor fact. But the fact was, and the myth
was, and they endure together.

This is written particularly to you.
Remembering, I shiver again as on that day
taking small comfort from our day as it is.

PROMISE

Sharp as hard-edged mineral that light
flaked off a hawkish Bay
shrewdly nipping air through the driver's window.
Covert roads turn their back on the coast,
shrug shoulders knowingly.
They begin handling you up into their hills
from lagoons and not as yet fully
reclaimed swamps or outreaching market gardens.
Newly ploughed loams on bits of flats carry
silvery snail-slime of latecome frost
of which there's more climbing
from seal to blue metal.

Wild peach and plum blossomings are still
tentative, willow budding less firmed
above the river, then creek, then stream, old
fashionedly, pure. A sense of cresting
into some Promised Land . . . credit
pioneers with that same sense, remembering

also eminently the Prophet returned from exile
hereabouts, to a stiffnecked rebellious folk
saying "This rock is one Table cast out of my hand"
and "That rock is the other Table I have thrown down",
those tables of covenant and testimony.
Then he went up on to a high place, towards promise
saying 'For mischief did he bring them out,
to slay them in the mountains, and to consume
them from the face of the earth?'
He set fire to the fern.

SMALL SONATA

1

Somewhere in this excited month a not so young
Maori confronts a northern face,
bluff stony hillside spill where few sheep
may safely graze. He's heir to responsibilities
more than he claims land for. Something tries to get
remembered by holes like eyes which are caves
from a long way back, darting out instead of telling glances
birdlike voices which are hard to hear.
They message him *You have people, commitments.*
To stare that slope square in the eye he must
look south—that's where spirits came from,
journeying, committed, body of the land.

Then sighing, he goes indoors to his wife
trying for sympathy. Glimpses himself, a stranger.
The night now, conjecture—Is the night excited?
The cliff face—Is that bluff withdrawn, apart?

His hungry sheep look up and are ill-fed.

2

Who at the end of another day
(the fall when any darkness finally is equal
to any feeling season) which she thinks of as another
autumn, who fronts a telltale mirror
like a clown in some version of *Enfants du Paradis* or
                    La Strada
tiredly to peel away her accomplished, accommodated
mask which she looks like, deadpan?
And slumps, brooding responsibly, herself alone?

They are like and like, together and apart.

3

Together and apart. She disparages her body
which is dear to him and speaks her language.
He's seldom been on good terms with his body.
They go inside, unmasked. Two lonely bodies lie
conversationally, together. Together, and together

24

they make their brief candle flare against
obligatory darkness, its onset, excited.
Upon a bed signifying
nothing much but working shadows, nothing
much but felicity. That we are and what we are
is possible. These lives are poor players about
fact which hides in some cave enduring (O my dear one)
stubbornly, as a northern face, as true
as fable, as apocrypha.

MOUNTAIN STOP

Downhill what's left of the Armed Constabulary patrol
men don't stand to arms, not wake their beat.
Long (they sleep late) are laid aside
the State Highway, who were definitively overtaken
by ambush. It's not like
                              Christopher
Perkins did or would have wanted to paint it:
but visibly, no kumara godstone
puts it at disadvantage, this enclave
among mountains which one habitually invents
peopled by enduringly children of mists.

North of where I came from
stones which have to sort with gods are roughcast,
toppling but not quite cast down
hill or dale, churches there preempt any
risen ground made to stand
over
any prospect—uplifted flat, the church takes
it, commands outlook, sect with sect, but
here in these hills is this site

which could stand *in loco parentis*
(Father, the first Father taught, forgive)
the dominant is reading from left to right
hotel/store/would you believe motel
                              superior to
a battered kainga of Tammy boar, rough Clydesdale,
junked Oldsmobile, kids loosed from schooling,
overweight kuia and slippered kaumatua
heaving up and easing down the grade
which takes them to/from the haulout
where MOW and Forestry tank up
in front of the post office general store tearoom
comfort station. Inside's
an impressive armoury fixed out of reach on the walls:
a long Lee Metford, carbines, muskets,
some exotic Arabian or North West Frontier weaponry,
a few handguns padlocked and stapled
Try to make talk about them, and get the brush off.
The boss man doesn't want to talk,
"That's only the half of them. There's more out back"

as he flipflops off to see that the boys in front
aren't milking the pump. Rain begins pock
marking a long puddle.

One thing for sure, Turuki isn't going
to ride through here again; he's been dead
a while since, somewhere over behind Ohiwa.
Things aren't better than they were?
No way. No way at all.

HOLE IN THE GROUND

Walk out to the ocean mark,
away from language. Hightide noon crouches
browbeaten, sliteyed. We do not recognise
the terms of our occupation,
what they imply. A background noise
wholly fails to overcome another
order, a dimension, of silence.

Breakers are not stopped from falling,
blustering or brawling rank on rank.
Slog inland, through the valley's big mouth,
recording
pulse of insects and the rocky creek.
You leave behind language, like dead shells
an incompetent syntax, a register
unresponsive. How shall I know
where I stand, until I say what I see?

Made deaf by excess of light,
a colonist's house, last farm, road's end,
tires any phrase, itself historical fact
leaning tonguetied towards an inarticulate
feeble macrocarpa. The tree tilts
towards the house. Nobody was at home.
Cattle dogs slept, a muddle of black,
white and tan, on the washhouse verandah.
The tractor did not speak.

Unsophisticated downfall,
soil faces along the beach, cut back
by aggressive weathering, show rubbish
layers of occupation. Up the coast
archaeologists are digging. Fragments
will not yet shape themselves
as discourse. A grassy headland
slides the remains of palisades down
the gradient which becomes a meadow,
all lupin, crossed by the creek's meanders.
Storms have crabbed bushes, littered
with driftwood to the foot of a rise
on which fall bits of shacks,
a flaking stove, frame of an outhouse
passionately used to near extinction.

Yellow admirals, little blues and day
flying moths speculatively cloud
the stream's precincts. Above an imitation
weir, where you abandon the bay flats,
the valley begins as glen or dale,
further darkly tightens and is a gorge
overhung by feral peaks and birds'
questioning crying,
which we no doubt misconstrue.

Cattle wander there. The creek lopes round
a flat stage with a fell steep behind;
opposite, cliff sheer to a stream bed of slabs.
Gross bulk of silence, bloodily oozing,
taxes unspoken queries. They bear upon
you, heavy as dialect, an alien grammar.

On that flat is a scar, six or eight feet deep,
not naturally straight. The spoil was
thrown mainly on the north side.
No conceivable function as defence,
incredibly long for a saw-pit,
not feasible as a cattle dip, wrong
location for building a canoe,
too wet for storage, without sign
that it was an oven . . . you tire
conjecture and query. Finally,
guess that it is anomaly,
a taro trench (some plants are *in situ*,
which may be misleading) of a kind
that Buck, for one, never saw in this country
but describes for islands beyond the Line.
That hardly helps. We do not follow

the terms of our occupation.

PIVOTING

around Taratara's several
bulk journeying is from one well defined high
way to another highway, detoured to travel
south by dint of heading north connecting
across country,
　　　　　　I do this because I love you,
you understand? You trust me, you are singularly
patient—longsuffering too, on this road taken
on trust, heat- and age-warped (along this track
Hongi went to whistle up his deadly wound
from ambush) and dung-spattered, when you've turned
your back on all that muscled heave and toss
which is Taratara from this point of view and that,
outcrop and fell, a geo logical fancy's flight
always taking off but never getting airborne, over
solidly grounded, stubbornly irreducible
fact: I'm not looking out for fable
or fortune, spinning the wheel
　　　　　　　　　　　where hard yacker is
what Hongi's heirs were left, and Ameria said
"Let's do up the meeting house!" so they did
so, then "Let us give the house a new name" so
they did, calling the house Te Aroha.
The promised land is further on,

desirable peaceable kingdom (the road shared
with freerange hoggets, Shorthorn steers,
some ponies, between cattlestop and cattlestop)
which isn't freehold or for all its lack in fencing
public domain, being only nine
hundred and ninety-nine years lease but near
idyllic Theocritean passage,
　　　　　　　　　　slab outcrops well
grassed between down to a stream which becomes
a river and rises into forest, but it can't
last. You return to sanity, which is flat,
prosaic. I do this because I love you,
I want to show you
　　　　　　　before we get back to the river
which for some while is splendid but has

30

a rough history, then spins into a mangrove
ridden prose before we reach
a many timbered ghost town (I have been
here before but won't find my way again
readily out of) to fetch the ferry, and cross
over. Either side, it's love and kind, of faith

[Handwritten annotations:]

tangled + boring?

Interpolation

styx imagery.

why 'fetch' instead of 'catch'

alliteration + assonance

Preps

layered [repetition = embedding]

missing obj.

SYLVIA

Sylvia! Sylvia! the activist/feminist poet
protested,
Here is Sylvia, this is She, obedient to
inscrutable lore. Sylvia is
cousin to a sow goddess. Well, we all know
what troubles are in cozenage. You tell me,
I'll tell you: I was in love with Sylvia
until she turned into a parable not for a just
good metamorphic cause,
something paradigmic instead. She had to prove
a point, and a point beyond that.

It's not always easy to love a pig.
Once I loved a pig pretty much like you can love
a cat, at first sight. She was Dinner, her sister was
Christmas; their father was a Captain Cooker,
their Mum was Tammy. God, they were ugly,
but lovable. Up the same valley was
Sylvia
          oh what indeed was she
that any swain commend her. She was pure
white, she was a Saanen
nanny. Her daughter was Luna.
They played tricks like hidey-go-seek
especially at milking time.
They shat delightedly their little goat pellets.
They wouldn't have anything to do with common
goat clans roaming the hills about.
They did not want to be metaphors for any
good causes. They were
themselves
             entirely, squinting over bushes to see
if anyone had found them out and I shall not let
them enter into politics, not
                      Sylvia, not Luna
while any day darkens and it's past
time for milking, time for bedding down.

LEGEND OF SARA'S GULLY

Miss Sara Milhall cast her eyes about.
Little she saw she liked, saw that but rarely.
On men, on women, brutal, bland, devout,
She looked, though no wise chanced on any dearly.

From fine community she passed away
To coarsegrained solitude, if yet not fully
Alone she housed herself subsistent, day by day
Queening it Crusoe-style in Sara's Gully.

She had the free birds and some few wild beasts,
Selected trees to talk with or to chary
Night winds stood conversational. Heady yeasts
Her teatrees brewed, no thing was ordinary

In Sara's crude demesne, her mate the least
Of all, bedfellow, bon vivant, mad raconteur,
Humorous, appetitive, staunch male Beast
Only part way domesticate—you demur

At such a matching? Sara did not so,
District gossip sedulously attested.
Where Sara went, Roland essayed to go.
His faith in her was totally invested,

Their lives quite intricate. Did she (you wonder)
In fondest moment murmur in his ear
"Ohhh . . . I could eat you!" He, craven of thunder
Omenly muttering their hills, "I could tear

You limb from limb!" frenzied, prognosticate.
This pillow sweetness, happenstance endeared.
Let lightnings blaze, stormed beaches fulminate,
The two were one. Then Sara disappeared.

In Time's due season people came to search.
Proprietorial, sleek Roland had them in,
Companion, guide, with many a manly lurch
His portly swagger, he, who long coursed thin,

Rank, lantern-jawed, avid—nowhere a sign
To tell of Sara more. Desperate the surmise
Which started to them, of outcomes condign.
They looked on Roland loathsome whose mild eyes

—Brutal, bland, devout—looked back, whose chaps
Champed thoughtfully, and frisked his agile tail,
Teetered his trotters, winked at them perhaps,
Was gone. Dreadfully those hills wail

On pelting nights these far years after, cold
Struck those who hear. An otherside intent
Silence stains parts of Sara's Gully, you'll be told,
As though they listen, locked in their dissent.

MOVEMENTS FOR COASTAL VOICES

1

Every manjack among them swung
his head after the one way, one fashion
as word passed around,
whispering (very nearly not to get heard)
"Over there is shining
the River of Water of Life", then sighed
into proceeding, some in file,
some, ruggedly independent, out of step
towards the river
and went down, the foremost, right to their knees
when they came to the shore.
Shells were before them, white and plain
as oldfashioned hymns singing back
gulf and ocean from reefs. From one islet, across
sandy flat spaces in parts sky-blue.

Recessional, the trees called
also their familiar sea, to enter
evening's channels, to resume
estuary mudflats which they entailed.
Herds of mangroves browsed a shallow
riverine estate. They were not swarthy
or garbled as tribes of the sandbar isthmus.

2

Circuit one estate: this was,
of a man of Irish family
(soldier, explorer, politician
disadvantaged) sometime governor in three
colonies, the Victorian
imperialists' Great Pro-Consul.

We were/are all of us
alienated. That's how we belong.
He was deaf, deafened by such distance—

out there, if you took a firm line
you'd fetch no landfall until
Chile. Think of that now! after
an afternoon at the old German hotel upriver,
pub and museum of a folk.

This was their cargo's way,
crooked as a founder's motives.
This distance which you swallow at a gulp—
it was their distance.

3

He stood on ceremony, like his trees
deaf to nuance yet knew mainly how the breeze
shaped. A bishop was his friend.
He parted from his wife in Valparaiso?

If you sailed out from this grove on its impulse
to abandon hold on a shoreline, flying
by emotions scintillant as local parrots,
you might well arrive at Valparaiso.

Gathering, among vines, burgeoning
dialects, language of entrepreneurs,
migrants from the states of being Germany.
Listen hard enough, you will not quite
hear them, feature in history.

He became a crust.

Political analysts should travel to touch
barks of these pohutukawa and tall manuka.
They are his comment. As, for Texans,
insight may signal to them from sundown
catching the pose of welcome junipers,
Mexico still dazzingly unsubdued.

4

A visiting Professor, of German;
his wife, expert in Celtic.

They walk, where there are tides,
They gather, shells which are not fossils.

5

Who could have foretold this?
Why, of course, no one. In the gloom

under the canopy of those tough
(in some sense, Mediterranean) leaves
to see ahead already wasn't easy.

Last daylight was elsewhere. Going
towards some part of its domain seemed
like projecting, extrapolating
an at best only moderately significant
thesis, from too little evidence.
Assured, light was aloof, remote.
Nobody was certain at all of the time,
how much we had left. Above our heads and the trees',
another dimension, reflective, differing
quality, more overtone to words spoken
than any help to see by. Under
foot, guide line of doctrine roughly
worked out, the ingrained ruts, cart track
from here to nowhere in particular, served us,
to a reasonable end. Taking the track
as granted, the lady from Texas was
saying, "Back home, our land lies
over the old Comanche Trail. Wagons
cut wheel ruts, where we have freshwater
springs. That's uncommon—" when

6

flashing like insight, parakeet arrived.
They flew in couples, threading branch
to branch, touching colours from
one or another tone of the overhang
or stroked a moment into blazing.

Astonishing, so fast they were economy,
apt and stylish. Startling, right
as a best scholar's glosses,
as little significant.

They were rosella from Australia.
We/they were/are alien, learning
the land's ways, to accommodate branch
with branch. *Der Erdenkreis ist
mir genung bekannt* . . . another
politico of a petty state might put

that line in a philosoph's mouth,
not to discredit; this is the stance
of exile. Where, surprising
birds to unpredictable passage,
voices
(almost you cannot hear them, imposed
on distance, steep as salt air's last burning)
exile speaks, reflective.
Stefan George's friend, going blind
in his old age, resting his hand on
a fig tree, murmuring *Thou* . . .
and I, also, a few miles only from here.

7

" —to have springs, of fresh water."

READING THE MAPS   AN ACADEMIC EXERCISE

All grid co-ordinates on this sheet are in terms of
false origin

Today when I was leaving you were gone
to the Library, hunting. So I couldn't say
what I wanted to say. No matter.
At nine I phoned about the mice and rats
which infest us, and departmental cats.
Are they procurable or not? No matter.

On the wall in front of my table are four
map sheets of Hokianga. One weakly faded,
the main part of a research scheme gone
mainly down the drain. Even when bought
it did not tell the truth (if truth I sought)
about that district. Some roads were gone

already, some were petered out to tracks,
some only projected. I quibble. It was truth
I pressed after to the blazing four
dusty points of the local compass, ground
by ground hunting for Mahimai and found
how legend bred him still, not one but four,

five or more versions of his Life and Times
in their ways different but yet held true for some
around those parts. They've not roads, mere tracks
in scrub or scruffy bush, beaten, halfway lost,
uncertain where they go, or stay. What cost
to follow them? What gains? Tracks are just tracks.

Or legends of them, getting nowhere much;
otherwise, fictions of any parish's mild dreams
mounted towards a future where times
would not work out of joint. Those sad dreams ailed
materially, the vision in them failed,
sailed off like so much junk caught up in Time's

hard-driving westerlies or blustering tides,
dumped among mangroves, slumped like driftwood on water
frontages. "The tourist will find much

to interest him, from . . ." From here to there,
hunting or haunted. Finding, found out where
roads disappear or don't amount to much.

Like schemes which I may think of, truth to tell.
No matter—no, that isn't true. Dusty, bitter
our ways work out, crudely move like tides,
nonetheless turn; comes turnabout in flow
and ebb, they matter. Down at the Head glow
finely the dunes. Promise still rides the tides.

☆

TO GIVE A GRID REFERENCE ON THIS SHEET

PAY ATTENTION TO LARGER MARGINAL FIGURES AND TO THOSE PRINTED ON THE FACE OF THE MAP VIZ $_8$30				
Point 270′ Rawhia				
East			North	
Take west edge of square in which point lies and read the figures printed opposite this line (on north or south margin) or on the line itself (on the face of the map) Estimate tenths eastward	10 5		Take south edge of square in which point lies and read the figures printed opposite this line (on east or west margin) or on the line itself (on the face of the map) Estimate tenths northward	42 6
East	105		North	426
Reference 105426				

Now I know where I stand, where I stood.
Within limits. All grid coordinates on this sheet are
true only in terms of false origin.

☆

Leave the highway just past a store
almost opposite this shortcut through the gorge.
You want to bear west beyond the store,
back of the district high school. As you go
you raise an abandoned church (which is here)
with a small marae. Shortly, the river.
Follow its bank for a bit, until
a farmer's yard, between the cowbail and pigpens.
So drive slowly. You'll need to.
The map says the road ends there. Not true.

You are now right under a stone face.
See the quarry sign? Drive
into the quarry, keeping to the hill side
(because of a fall on the other hand to the river).
You skirt a shoulder. Look for an unformed road
lifting suddenly, steep. But get over the crest,
you're on top of packed sand.
Carry on to the Head. You cross
the old tramway which used to go up to
the Harbour, remains of the one time main road
to gumfields (south of the river and this next
river) out from the edge of the Forest. It went on
down the coast, then climbed inland on the line
of a Maori trail. Of course, the map doesn't
say anything about that. Maps can

tell you about what is supposedly present.
They know little about what's past and only
so much about outcomes. They work within
tacit limits. They're not good at predicting.
If everything is anywhere in flux
perhaps we may not read the same map twice.

A DEFENCE OF RYME

*Nor must we thinke, viewing the superficiall figure of a
region in a Mappe that wee know strait the fashion and
place as it is. Or reading an Historie (which is but a Mappe
of men, and dooth no otherwise acquaint vs with the true
Substance of Circumstances, than a superficiall Card dooth
the Seaman with a Coast neuer seene, which alwayes
prooues other to the eye than the imagination forecast it)
that presently wee know all the world, and can distinctly
iudge of times, men and maners, iust as they were.*
                                        Samuel Daniel

THE BOOK OF THE ROAD

Out on A 61 for Ripon
Left at Ripley on B 6165
  to Pateley Bridge

41

Pateley Bridge through Grassington
  on B 6265, to connect
B 6160, through Kettlewell, Starbotton
  and Buckden
Turn left at Buckden and follow
  Langstrothdale Chase to Hawes
  (not numbered)
Hawes-Bainbridge on A 684, cross to
  Askrigg and on (no number) to
  Castle Bolton

Have lunch there?

Castle Bolton, over Redmire Moor to Reeth
Reeth into Arkengarthdale
Turn right beyond Langthwaite over
  Scargill High Moor to meet A 66
Right again, to B 6277, there left to
  Barnard Castle

Allow time to see castle, medieval bridge and
  inn where Dickens wrote *Nicholas Nickleby*
  (so the Treasures book says) and esp.
  Bowes Museum (if open??)

From Barnard Castle backtrack on B 6277
Watch for turn off (unnumbered) to
  Egglestone Abbey
(Have tea there or in town?)
Then follow River Tees to get back to
  A 66 for Greta Bridge (isn't that Dotheboys
  Hall?)
Carry on A 66 to Scotch Corner, down A 1
to turn off on A 59 through Knaresborough

NOTE: Roman road beyond Oughtershaw on way
       to Hawes and site of fort at Bainbridge
       From Greta Bridge A 66 follows a Roman
       road (no name)

☆

We may not read the same map twice,
especially where sands are on the move.

42

I speak loosely because thinking
not of a map's ineptitude but of
some shiftless nature which is prior.
Maps merely feign to represent the case.
Shiftless? A shifty case, more like,
unsure in its election as well as
in its origin, in its ground
of being as well as in its becoming—
neither works any way too well
for this instance. Are we not assuming
that what one has here to purport
to use as an example will survive
scrutiny? Somehow, has survived?

You follow me: I talk of what we have
and have not, of a sandhill lake
which comes and goes. Or maybe, came and went
since when I was last probing there
forestry men and engineers intent
on reform were then debating
how best to right an aberrant nature.

Their maps could not properly cope
with it. It was offence to natural
justice, natural right, and law.

It came and went. Worse, it was essential
when not existent. Boundaries
tentatively it had, often flouted.
It had? Check my legal fiction.
Rather, they had. Sometimes three lakes flaunted
themselves, sometimes two, or only
one, or none. Not only sands were on the move,
the lake dissolved, moved, reappeared,
will dwindle, again quicken. In remove
a presence, in presence a fact
substantial, insubstantial form
no less? This play with arid words,
dry as lake beds where cloudy midges swarm
until extinguished, the dunes made
to conform to rational order and
rabid, but useful, their surgent pines
established turn to increase wayward sand.

Something we know lost, gained by that.
Then how, best right aberrant nature?
Terms of reference not precise,
you guess, we may not read the same map twice.

☆

REFERENCE

On the sheet in front of me on the wall
two sections REFERENCE.

The section on the left has

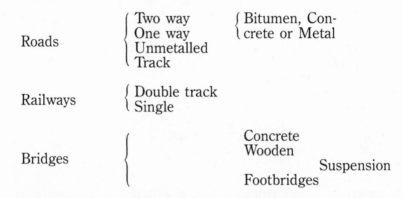

Roads   { Two way   { Bitumen, Con-
         { One way   { crete or Metal
         { Unmetalled
         { Track

Railways   { Double track
           { Single

Bridges   {   Concrete
              Wooden
                        Suspension
              Footbridges

with some other things about Main Electric Transmission lines,
Distribution lines, Conventional spacing, Wooden poles and Actual
positions

Pylons   No

I am leaving out all the signs for them, you understand? Also,
anything to do with telephones, tramways and the distinctions of
Principal from Smaller stations.

The section on the right has

Keys to bush, trees, plantations, scrub, scattered scrub, hedge
or short row of trees, fence (prominent), swamp, mangrove, drain,
sand, shingle, cliffs & terraces, stop bank, rocks, building,
church, cemetery, windmill, radio mast, additional clues for
trigonometrical stations with permanent signals, spot heights in

44

feet above mean sea level, sketch contours at 100′ intervals, and
bits about post and telegraph services. Outside the limits of the
code are two other notes, how to recognise a pa, and rock
outcrops with large boulders.

Given all that you should be able to operate
within or without prescribed or designated limits.
You may yet have to go to the wall.
How was I ever able to find my way there?

☆

HOW TO GET BACK BY MAGNETIC BEARINGS

True North, now, that is one thing.
This another, how to get back
(wherever that was) magnetically drawn
to harbour. Instruct me, all I ask,
instruct me how—this *plus*, or lack
as *minus,* evidently apply—to unmask
a not altogether dissembling
map? True, is true of false origin.

TO CONVERT A	TO CONVERT A
MAGNETIC BEARING	GRID BEARING TO A
TO A GRID BEARING	MAGNETIC BEARING
ADD G–M ANGLE	SUBTRACT G–M ANGLE

TO OBTAIN G–M ANGLE
add the Annual Magnetic Change
multiplied by the number of years
since 1965 to the G–M angle for 1965
1°=60′
Annual Magnetic Change +3′
G–M Angle for 1965 16°30′ for
the Central Grid Line of this sheet

You may not read the same map
twice. On such least point we may agree
without implying more. Or may we? Add or subtract,
something's still to be read as before
contemptuous of cartography
as of art or art's surrogates, its sniffling poor

relations which I ape, thumb at lip
lacking bearing, puerile seen-through act

so you say. As you say.

☆

SYMBOLS

I cannot see our land clearly.
It comes and goes because covered with symbols.
Isn't this symptom of a psychotic state?

Take England now. In England I was given
to hold in my hand a necessary guide to
SYMBOLS USED ON THE MAPS, to hold as I was driven.
'O take fast hold'—that's Sidney, in *CS 32*.

Eleven different sections of symbols on one sheet,
twenty of them in one section. Here's from
another:
       Castle or house with interesting interior
       Abbey, priory or other ecclesiastical
         building (usually in ruins)
       Parish church
       Castle or house in ruins
       Archaeological monument
       Garden (usually attached to private house)
       Botanical gardens
       Zoological gardens

but no *Interesting church*. Interesting churches are
in Symbols Used on Town Plans, another section.

Another section, of another life.
Here I am told how to find a *Frontier post*.
I shall go down to the river which may be

demented. I shall go on hoping to cross over.
Perhaps this is a frontier. We have crossed
frontiers before this.

46

Here is a sheet of paper. Write on it for me.
Go on, write on it. Why do you write *No.*?
What number do you mean?

☆

LEGEND

I

this landscape landfall.

II

A map so new you wouldn't read about
it, a loop road which hadn't been built
in hill country behind Tokomaru Bay.
Way forward proved the way back.

Like a one track mind it pressed as far,
died under a mount, a none too significant
mound. So have we all, well truly spent.
Well, there was the mount. On its round

emphatic the bull, who rose to design.
His neck arched, the masculine pouch,
his weapon cooling, out to prove
that way forward is the way back

III

where maps may need a change in legend for

IV

this masculine landfall/landscape

and seascape. Together, your un-
certainty in seeing, grit and spray
confronting or bedevilled, those dun
sands drove at berm and cliffs while away
in their distance sea leagues with
the land's league collogued were one,
classically distant. Could you well say
how far in space or time you were astray

from plainjane rivermouth, that plebeian

rivermouth beyond the quarry,
beyond the mundane?
                        On the wall
fronting me I pinned, years ago, a wry
black *toro* from a Spanish bottle
to further esemplastic
legend's proclivity
for becoming and *there* would do as well
as anywhere, near Mahimai's burial
place. As chance worked, it's not very

far from the beach where (December
'69, was it?) the skyline
crests learned how to break with their severe
old puritan habit, its condign
bearing, stood—preliterate,
hieratic—risen clear
above confusion the young bulls in line,
preternaturally clear. They define
and redefine what you perhaps swear

is land that cannot wear myth's host
plausibly, an unlikely stock.
Surveyors missed them running out the coast
but legend needs. We are what dreams shock
briefly to become; this you heard
long since. Then where, at cost,
shall we amazed be forced to press the rock
channel deep, final, face him who will lock
and batten on us? Fictive, will most

prove fact? Way forward is way back
baffling to wayward plan or chart,
a maze the end and origin, track
not made good though trick you got by heart
sorely. I speak of the Minotaur
at the heart of us, the black
kruptos, that animates each crafty art?
All pay him tribute, kill him off, and start
to run his course again shiftless, bleak

48

V

as fallen masculine scape tumbled
headlong, Sprawls, fold on fold. Heaves,
scarred hide. Promise still rides.

South and east they have fire by night
in their skies. Here, to the north a mast,
a television repeater station catches
signals. What sign/signal/symbol for
the Muse? Perhaps

VI

on a hilltop a crossbred Jersey sire.
His progeny champ below, mouse-coloured
in their rat run. He bellows, hefts clods.
They caper excited, I am shit-scared

clinging then to one strand of No. 8
fencing wire the guard rail of a swing
bridge over a creek, just discovered
that several planks ahead are missing.

The bulls come gathering either end and
as well as my pack there's all the camera gear.
He bellows and bullocks. They collect, they dance.
We are offered, in season. In season
not at the dark heart, out in the open

VII

are taken, being promised. *As/Was*
Mahimai and probably Rutherford
(if that was his name) who disappeared
in a cloud of bullshit, who said he spent
ten years of himself back of Tokomaru.

That was the first season I went looking
for Mahimai and Rutherford, sidetracked
into hunting after graveyards' wooden
headboards, their iconography lost style.
About them maps are reticent.

I swung between: a family burial ground,
and the Wesleyans' plot. With those boards

which we cannot read and the grave of
their millenarian teacher, Heke's tohunga
Papahurihia. The vates? They deny

VIII

but we need more to the legend, and for

☆

A QUESTION OF SCALE

To bring it all to scale, the given
   is 1:63360, 1 inch to 1 mile,
     and is outmoded.

That, given. Also false origin
   is given as base from which we work, almost capable
     until outmoded.

To bring it to scale I was driven
   or drove headlong, taking whatever a telltale dial
     on an outmoded

dashboard said was nearly true of *Then*
   and *There,* the literal. Metaphor too, and parable
     long since outmoded.

Reading Mandelstam in a coffee shop,
taking a break between one and another town.
Surprised: realise, not one or other is obviously monstrous.
Dry-eyed women out there, are they
actually trying to find husbands?

The Art Gallery (this is a Monday) is closed.
Fortune telling is against the law;
anyhow, gone out of fashion.
If the Pony Club has right of way along the main
    drag, it's for a good cause.

Whoever here is wounded has neither streetcar
nor Army recourse. Getting out of town's a puzzle,
although mainly one way routes. There are said
to be by-passes. People who used to play
hippies or flower children in camouflage gear
wave, call from car to car "Don't worry, we'll be back!"

You guess, an elderly twosome at a next table are
    widows, killing time
overlooked by buggy wheels, bicycles, pack
saddles, species of memento mori.
This is not Voronezh. Not 1937.

AFTER ONDRA LYSOHORSKY

Dark fictitious islands
rising like wooded mountains
from smoking prospect, which is
reasonably familiar.

As a seaway. And gallowsscape, that too!
Point beyond Colville, quarry
which serves monumentally funeral
masons. They launch their granite freights.

Upon the wine-dark mysteries. Seas swerve,
they charge intemperately not pithead
gear, not blast furnaces' hellmouth,
indeed no. Not everything is wrecked.

By machinery, only abetted. Here this
looms, just homely enough for a whole
but local fellow if in the mood
to venture his abyss. He goes mouthing.

His sea hellishly portentous. He jerks
himself off the pierhead defiant.
In summer haze we are likely mistaken.
A penal arm dangles our gulf surely.

Yet not a Hanged Man. Only some burden
for a float below. We take the case wrongly.
Little everyday deaths are possible
one way or other. And how easy.

The crane's arm answers. Winds
are turbulent, islands malformed,
mountains aloof, the Christmas tree
groves dense with boding. Colonia—

their old resistant human
preoccupation. Your man emerges from
a grove, into lucidity eminently
sceptical. Still, he is preoccupied.

With presence? Yes, that within
the groves. With proclivity,
for investing your reasonable
familiar prospect? That also.

PASTERNAK: THEME WITH VARIATIONS

Life, my sister, does not freely issue
any safe conduct, dossier, itinerary
or catalogue raisonné, to poets
last of all. They thrive scandalously

out of kilter, getting things rightly
wrong way round, who will see things
from every corner of the eye
squarely. We run, Lydia, out of tune,

out of time. It was the future killed
off Mayakovsky, I tell you, and insist
I do not offer memories to memory
of Rilke. How may I? He gave them me.

When we shall be translated, we exist.
The poet is what they who love him
make him, within their limits, by their
forgivings. Their pity, too? Surely,

their charity. We must be kind,
because, being alive; if not kind, then
at least long suffering. When I was
a boy in Marburg people murmured

Existence precedes Essence. How can
you run a straight line through trivia?
Rilke tried: Venezianischer Morgen,
Spätherbst in Venedig, San Marco . . .
the lines are good, but tug against the line.

It's truer what you make me say:
I woke, first light, looked out, and saw
how 'Venice swam in water' like
'A sodden pretzel made of stone.'

Existence is (my dear) like this, like that.

PASTERNAK: THE MAKING OF A POET

1

First, Mama at her piano, then Scriabin
six years absent was come home to Moscow.
Pasternak played him things written
while the Master stayed abroad.
Cigar smoke swayed below a gilded salon ceiling,
silver glittered, misty pancakes, of course
a samovar whispering like a snake.
His hosts did their best to make him easy.

Music, the end and his beginning.
Scriabin kindly was encouraging.
"Borya, Borya," he confided, "does it matter
if you haven't perfect pitch?
Wagner, Tchaikovsky, did they have perfect pitch?"
It's what piano tuners need,
composers or executants—his arm pressed round
the youngster's shoulders—do they need?
Discussed, some arts of composition
("Do not improvise") and worth
simplicity commands.
                          Simplicity was why
Boris had chosen to go in for Law.
"But never! Never!" This couldn't be. "You must
change your life tomorrow!"
Boris enrolled next day
'in the historico-philological'
to study in philosophies.

He ran drunk with Moscow, markets, alleyways,
houses which stood up singing three-part pieces,
with prospects, distances, choral peasant beasts,
horses which were string trios,
orchestrated movement of night walkers.
Getting ready, to suspect he might be free.
Marvellous, what happened at street corners.

2

Sometime once, was years and years ago,
everything summer in a journeying forest
blinded by sweat-stained leaves.

They had to rest the horses
until, shaking reins, they left behind
a German on a roadside bank. Perhaps—
you'd think almost certainly—he waved
after them, disappearing into various lives
down longer dusty vistas.

About the time Scriabin went to—Venice?
They all loved Venice, were always leaving for—
a book fell off its shelf. Boris was helping
Mother dust and tidy.
                   Chance (he emphasises)
had nothing to do with picking up that
one (of them all, grey, faded, inscribed to Father)
book. He didn't like the poems
straight away, yet gradually they fell like water drops
on a porous stone, ready, to absorb, be worn,
won, made over. Then another volume,
same hand, to which a face
might be put, a gesture
under some weight of trees, Farewell!

Or greeting?
Doors opened, meaning friends.
Some were called paintings, a few were scores
much scratched upon and blotted; the tipsy lot
were ballads, lyric, an aborted epic.
Their knuckles, ways they had on tabletop or panel
sounding out truly Russian arts'
substantial pulse. If asked, "We are the Sirdards,
brothers, a company likeminded."
Also he was in love.

3

Between seasons he trudged a desert, of words.
He wasn't used to language. He spoke
keyboards, staves. Fifteen years without a lexicon,
what surprise that he should find
himself original? "I was doomed,
naturally. Like a man with a gammy leg learning
to walk, can he do anything but acrobatics?"
How do they learn to skate high up in Norway?

Admitted: Biely, Blok, pointed out where ice spread
thinly.
   How to a sultry attic overhung
by poplars, how chilled in fog,
rain, or driving snow (rooks busy at their own
abrasive motets) shambling corduroy sidewalks,
he was surely conducted as Orpheus,
Eurydice. Hermes went before,
in worlds of charms and snakebites
his name was Rilke.

4

Love raced ahead.
He grew by indirections, purposefully random,
shrewd-set angular to Others.
     Biography
simplemindedly can't pass as a diagonal
from some field's corner to its apposite.
Roads too, they have their wandering habit.
Creatures of impulse, may pause at Marburg
to guess at which way next, prodigiously
stepping it out with an otherwise forgotten
philosophe conveniently deaf in one good ear.
The head waiter at a cafe more decisive:
"You must leave tonight by the express
a few minutes after three." They drank to this,
a strawberry punch. What else?
All streets around had been used up.
Women would sew at windows as before,
nobody would be deceived.

5

Even stars over Venice are not same.
Street corners there, they can't tell right from left,
bridges turn into squares.
Immediately arrived he thought he saw
a face once seen, "I couldn't remember where,
moonlight plays tricks." Later he observed
people seemed strangely familiar.

6

Under the Constellation of the Guitar
palaces, churches, belltowers and dosshouses
went off like fireworks in a deluged ballroom.
Transparent horses thundered, guiltily rioting;
not sparks, but blue glass fragments fled their feet,
vanished in a lion's mouth.
City of slaves, and Pantaloon—the Austrians were
long gone home. When he woke,
not *Fürstlich verwöhnte Fenster,* his sill
was crammed with tins which housewives use,
creams, polishes, some dirty chalk.
A little kid was yapping to her grandma.
Wanting to change his room, was told, "Please
sir, don't interfere in matters of our family."
Moments waited for him in doorways,
along galleries. Accident, concord,
no place was ever empty or hard of hearing.
Stones reached up as high as rhetoric might.
Boris did things which eager tourists do,
envied the English. Studied paintings,
rode the waters, loitered.

Moscow was busy remembering 1812.

FIN DE LA BELLE ÉPOQUE: MISIA'S VIEW

On days that were at best only
halfway wet fat Indian Summer tears slowly
coursed her corner grocer's plateglass windows.

Belgian refugees arrived. They were ragged, gaunt,
scared stiffly doubled under nowise burdens
raucously toted, their defeat's leftovers.

If winds blew from right aspects families took
off for the Bois, to listen:
Papa would know, was that a cannonade?

A German aviator mounted Paris.
He dropped three bombs, one old woman died unnamed
beside a note she didn't quite latch on to—

'The German Army's at your door. There is
no choice but surrender.
                              Leutnant Heidssen.'

In bold checked shooting jacket the neighbourhood
antique dealer stalked his quai, rifle hoisted,
offering potshots at any aerial vandal.

Man must be steadfast to contend his values.

Misia who was in the know (knowing just how
badly things were going) persuaded
all closed couturiers to lend their vans.

She turned vans into ambulances,
confiscated linen, towels, whatever'ld serve
mutilés de guerre, from several hotels

and one establishment, l'Hôtel du Rhin,
she placed on twentyfour hour watch.
A Red Cross in herself was Misia, borne away to war.

Gorgeously she went, saying goodbye to her generation,
she in tweeds, her pale grey husband Sert knickerbockered,
his monstrous Kodak at the ready.

Iribe the designer took the Mercedes' wheel.
Beside him Cocteau, bickering, for whom Poiret ran up
a stunning male nurse's uniform . . .

                                    Franco-Britannic
ladies who plained and purled at woolly unders
for kilted hairy Jocks were not allowed
to see what newly fashioned men the vans brought back,
the great Merc at their head.

In Misia's apartment poets, painters, savants,
conferred together drawing up routes for convoys,
Men, even artists, should be steadfast.

Her aquariums were neglected. Fish floated belly up.
Saint-Saëns campaigned against all German music.
Along the Seine steamers played their searchlights
vigilantly upon the waves their traffic made.

DEATH IN VENICE: DIAGHILEV

Almost the last he said was "Promise me
you will always wear white."

Lifar told her how the mind had wandered:
first time he went abroad, his student nights and days,
going down the Volga, conquest of Paris,
all spilling out. He sang Tchaikovsky's *Pathetique*—
"That's what I've loved most, all my life."

Day broke as he died.
The sea was sheet metal, flaming, pure stagecraft.
Reflection washed his forehead.
Boris sprang across the bed, Lifar barked.
They bit, they ripped at clothes, they fought from wall
to wall. Difficultly
Misia and the nurse dragged them apart.

After a service with the Orthodox,
black gondolas, gilt angels sparkling, faceted
priests' voices over many jewelled waters.
At San Michele earth was wounded.
Lifar and Kochno crawled on hands and knees
to the graveside, one tried to throw himself in
with his master. End of an epoch, August '29.

Misia scarcely noticed Wall Street crashed.
She'd troubles of her own, with bed and board.

SEVENTY YEARS

Someone determined the highway should
lie as it does, allowing you pull
over

beside a gas station and an antique
shop with prices hiked altogether
too high.

They between them confect a placebo,
to topical provincial unrest
which is of spirit,

of those who misplaced cannot think
big enough. They make a placename only
warranted

by roadmaps, comfortless comfort stop.
Cloud, rain, more cloud—over your shoulder's
inevitably

the Mountain, seen or unseen, resolute,
focal. Weathers like roads depend, testify to.
Across

paddocks beyond the rail line is where
the old road went like a habit, outgrown.
It's there

as much as was used to hang out most
mornings, bringing the cream to offload, pick
up yesterday's

papers and local gossip, a dead dairy
factory. Its facade has twin mimic peaks,
one face

weather-worn illegible, but the other
puzzlingly (in low relief) declares for

1914
TRIUMPH

which should be recorded before silenced
like the distant headstrong guns of August.
I fetch the camera.

get into shelter, plan the shot. The cocking
lever won't cock, film won't reel. The shutter's
jammed.

PLACE

Shocking, to realise how little you remember:
place—hamlet, village, township—either side of
tarmac which did not invite you to stop.

Side roads, true, side roads stepped back
into lives entirely reticent,
more than met the eye before they met fencelines
    and flat farm boundaries.

A shabby, an unpretentious, decency? As may be.
Does it seem smaller than it is?
Not that the name's unknown, but imagination has
to struggle hard to endow *this*
with consequence, given, in two wars
how many thousand men were camped, trained here?
Of them, no sign. Fields are desert.
Flocks may safely graze.

A memorial importantly stanced tells
this is sister to one similarly matter of fact in Flanders.
Earth was gravely hurt.
                  Improvident rains sweep,

you cannot see clearly, if, beneath an outskirt tree
a woman stretches her hands as though she weighed
something, yet what would that be? Perhaps a Muse,

they call to their sisters in outlandish tongues.
They bid each other, uncommonly gesturing.
Their ways, their choices, are always strange.

CLOSEDOWN

We who do not belong in and from
our distance watched while the town aged,
not promised to any Indian Summer.
From age, to ailing,
                however seawinds freshen
their houses are unbraced, their shops
more stocked with memories than current
goods. Everything was staked on
the Works, unjustified.
                  The Works allowed
to run down at last closed. A ghost town
in the making? It's not comfortable,
delaying.

What have we ever known about it?
    A couple of rightwing local Members we didn't
think much of.
    One young novelist of then promise set his first
novel up and down the slope: troubled faith,
                    unrecovered innocence.
    Years as a river port, fifteen wrecks,
all fairly humdrum.
    A Constabulary post, frontier fashion, freighting base,
another name in the second Taranaki campaign.

The main street is the main highway.
An oldest business looks out grimly,
    McSomething or other and Hunger, Est. 1878.

KLYNHAM

He lived at home with his Mum,
drank too much, played in bands about the district,
had (as you might say) an active imagination,
was (you can say that again) a character.
He didn't think much of people who took precautions.
He populated all these parts.

How much did the town notice him living
until he died, who switched their reference points?
The water tower, for instance, he reconditioned
like an old motor so it could take off
from (the borough's highest point) firmly grounded
stasis, eminently reasonable, entirely practical.
Now, what he imagined, it is.

Lace- and fretwork fronted pubs,
them he gave authority. The main street mall,
why, he foresaw this too, as well
bus terminal, walk-through, stock and station
agents' Japanese car and farm machinery mart,
Oddfellows and Buffalos lodges,
they're from his hand, memorial. Where
fictions end embarrassed fact starts up.

I'd like to hang about a while
but not for long. A block or two that way he made
a garage, gave it a car to service.
Maybe that car's still in the district
                                        a maroon
Auburn roadster, canvas-topped, twin chrome
exhaust hoses beautifully sneaking back
from the raunchy bonnet. The engine was
a Lycoming. They didn't build many of them,
only one came to this country, test driven
by Ab Jenkins at Bonneville, 104 m.p.h.?

Truly, I believe.

PERHAPS PARABLE PERHAPS POLITICS

All day, brilliantly chill day where
no wind however small, from hilltop
above us anybody could look over
what's otherwise faded distance into
distinct, ridge shapes away southerly
never before noticed, as well as what you might
predict, intimate folds in the Moehau range,
faintly tender loom of islands summer does not
rave about.
          We're on a downslope, pocketed,
weedridden in manners which real estate agents
call 'bush sections'. Over the fence
someone is burning; who wants to learn
nextdoor names? He has a fire out of sight.

Smoke rises through privet, matipo and willow strands.
It's pleasant, that blue through suitable screens.
All day ash falls, flakes, just so big, lightly.
They don't amount to anything, neither impose
nor disturb.
          Are these documents or garden spoils
which are burning? Perhaps, only variously
wasted lives. If we were to see the faces would we
at all recognise them?

BACKGROUND MUSIC (II)

Creatures of reasonable identity
kissed not by numbers leaning to the Other
responsibly, leaned
breasts into hands, heavy
enough as responsibilities—not likely that people
go lucky in latecome love, illjudged and
in a wrongheaded season, naturally.
Then, there, breasts were twin birds—
doves (they would, would they not, have
to be conventionally) settling, singing contrary
to commonsense, into care
readily, like paired birds lifting down
from some cote at Esterhazy, settling.

Without words for any language but need.

They came to hold, heard under
them, rhythm like complaint we ail of,
homecoming. Hands were accepting
whatever a girl sang about, kitchen maid
à l'hongroise of her time, of this place.

This unkind/kind state, of love,
tenderness, affection, lust, this painful
joy, indeterminate sadness, how welcome?
We are irrational identity. We are
wholly vulnerable.

OF SORTS

A sometime bloody ground where being ails.
This World, I count it not an Inn but an Hospital;
and a place not to live, but to dye in.

Suppose (as people say) God has not revealed
himself to the birds, to ask "What then, of that?"
The birds only? Why, not yet Felicity's disclosed
those twin set doves her breasts to even a most
fortunate young fellow, let alone laid bare
her cleft of generation, that sometime bloody ground
where being aches, prepared, impostumed,
importuned. Yesterday

I came away from the geriatric wards
where old ladies were laid to rest after
their lunching. The wards were still, sun courts
empty, corridors vacant and merely
one voice screaming *Why am I like this?*
Why am I like this? Why . . .
which faded, like distraction from a glass.

WAITOMO

Guides ask for silence, and have
no difficulty in getting their parties
to go quiet. At a dollar a head, nations
file underground. All shapes of age bow
their heads, step carefully after.
Go deep, go down to silence.

Bridal Chamber, and Cathedral,
play of fancy which wants to discover
limestone making metaphors, shadow likenesses
and shadow play. Here is Dog, there is
Camel. We call this the Modern Art
gallery, but go down
further, one more, a couple more flights.
A boat at a landing stage idles,
another will carry us, silently
animated through the grotto
where cannibal worms hunt, breed, age,
consume their partners, are consumed.

How this would have pleased Coleridge,
riding a verbless river, the dome,
darkness, glowworm haven
generously imitating, freely outdoing, stars.

I have been here before, without words.
After their climax of love people lie thus,
as though drifting dark waters, caverned.
If you speak, all the lights will go out.
Say nothing. She reaches for his hand,
he presses her finger. The boat slides
curving back to its landing.

A guide at the stage sweeps his lamp
over a pool. What is he looking for?

KIRITITEHERE

Western ocean's cunning, heaving against.
Hills inland (muscular, craggy as oldtime wrestlers) surge,
        grip their own weathers to them.
                                Downstream,
sluggish creeks fumble for course among
rhyolite hamlets, cabbagetree kraals, drift tenements
disputed by ducks and eels. District with a thin skin—
tap it, tomos break underfoot. There's more than meets
any storm's crazy eye.
                        Just after daybreak clans straggle
up-country, weatherbeaten, motheaten. Humpbacked
rangatira, wives, priests, entourage of nobodies, lug
their chattels away from the coast. Noone has told them
they were a hundred years dead. Of
evangelical ardour? That too, maybe; at least, in part.
No place to bring a lady, yet men proselytising brought
their wives, their catechists. Stepped canny.
                                        Why not
be wary? It's one thing to have missionary zeal.
Another, to huddle in a tent that wants to take off
after Victoria's peculiar century. At hand
a wild fig enclave is in turmoil
                        all night
with voices (they cannot count, they age sensibly
like compromise) you might swear to, confiding
how to a city-like lady *she is a creek that runs hard,*
runs clear dreaming herself body of the land,
caught between terror and ethos her own storm
wrestles with

                Never bird cried as your mouth knows
nor man so held to a good land as in your thighs
*you hold him—*where did this come from, a missionary
zeal? Between tremor and logos
                        her man slogs
away into wind and rain regardless, slights omen
or metaphysic, fries eggs and bacon. The fat spits.

WRITING ON THE WALL

Painted haphazard buttercup gold letters
on a receptive wall where bricks long since arrived
bone weary, their nails pensionable, that's
where it was, message which overlay contumely,
prayer, faded wishful thinkings—
YANKEE GO HOME, The NLF will sit at the Conference
Table, Fower Power Today, People not Personnel,
Make All Women Free, that's what they said
but this said
    Flying machines will never get off
the ground. They are doomed to fail. The bumblebee is
aerodynamically unstable.
      As improbable,
as not to credit, to mark that sound made by
a skirt, she folding it over a chair.
Unpredictable, modelling of hip, thigh, small of back.
Irrational, fingers taking hold of him towards her.
The fact is, humblebees do fly, suiting an inexplicable
    weather.

At such very same time
        fortuitous aliens shambled
about Britain's snowscapes. For them an old story
catchcried, Will our winter never end?
Any returning spring season was evidently unlikely,
against reason, against their senses which accumulated,
   older.
Then kerbside sycamores were black, bleak, as age.
A man might think he was a Victorian house almost
without tenant, yet where voices went backwards/
forwards weaving in trio in rooms upstairs
a forgotten foreign language, some grammar
which some time knew how to love. But things
changed, discernibly. (You could read what was written
on foursquare walls.) Daylight was longer,
aspens were new again.
      They began to make sounds
like whispers of cloth, folded over a chair
in half dark. Moonlight showed her like a tree,
as illogical, yet verity, of senses which put out new
leaf. Only a little was she like moonlight.

ONE SUNDAY ABOUT THE LONG RIVER

Walk me to Paradise Garden. It would
be an apple orchard—it is an orchard
without serpent or guile, no lost Eden, found
shining handsomely when all the more to tell
because not like this expected. You round a curve
to enter on discovery. We've been
here before, and the apples
themselves? They are, they have to be, Gala
as for days signally like this day.
But this day is, it is not like.

I am trying to find.

Over the road from the drive-in
a loft, in the loft an old A class keeler.
She was the squadron's pride. Elegantly,
disappears into the shed's darkness.
On three sides of her tenement trees bend
their rich heads. I am trying to say,
"A member of a sort, in wedding" we stand.
She is bridal white, still.

The packing shed/sales place is loft
too of another kind which rides above
lanes of water-wise tributaries, offering tidal
customs of the country as well as fruits.
They've made a modest museum without
comfortable words but comfort objects:
four stationary engines,
knowledgeable saws which dealt with native
trees, bullock gear, some simple crafts.

A simplest skill, that's what baffles me
to find, to say, all the more to tell
necessarily. Right, yes, of necessity
to tell: of what was, not like, entering
your darkness in a night before this day.
Conspires, to further. Contributes, to
sensible delight. Render to the day.

HIGH NOON AND AFTER

Vacant blue, altogether superior air
staring out of countenance, staring you down that high
noon which too shrewdly gathered what men were at
under the apple trees. We took fruits forbidden,
we shall be cast out of countenancing. Any man
his own mystery, we play at. Innocence
lost the garden too long ago, how the fruit tasted
forgotten. But may still say "We . . . ours" for
better or worse.
        In a dry season clouds came
not promising rain. I should like to have seen
the goddess, She who is Maid, Wife, Crone?
Or she who is Virgin, Astraea who bears
out of season a blazon of ripe corn?
Nothing of the kind.
          You want comfortable words
yet cannot spell a hawk from a handsaw?

Formerly a friend handy with visions would
wrestle with bull or with virgin and his fall tell
over. 'Man' he said 'is a walking grave. You must
keep the wound bleeding' until struck down.

Afternoon wore painfully thin
skinned, a shell of dearth. I was carapace, nothing
within but longing, displaced, urgent to say
"We . . . ours", comfortable words.

CHRIST CHURCH YARD, 1984

They shine through even a so damp and vision
limited late afternoon, competent,
confident, inwardly assured because knowing
people like us now or beforehand cannot/could not
afford them, expensive toys.
                      They ride
calmly, their big game outrigger arms tidily
ported, evident of talents for seeking and striking,
hunter killers whose moorings are
                              where
whalemen lay, and men of war.
Some, boated and landed, of them lie a little
uphill where their game was played out
about the church who went hand to hand as
rumbustious children might along with
the first white child born in the Bay (and in
the country?) but this one
was
before they contested church fences
hand in hand, or the men at war raked with cannonade
their church's walls.
                She lies behind
almost out of gunshot's reach,
who did not know of game or toy even the least
costly in whatever spirit.
                Margaret looks
at the grave of her great aunt three
(or four, or more?) times removed,
Anne Maria, whose father was Robert, her mother Charlotte,
who died in her ninth month, 1841.
Nox perpetua, perhaps, or *sunt lachrimae,* or
*O du, des Vaters Zelle/Ach, zu schnell erloschner
Freudenschein!* may not the Reverend
Robert have mused here? in a Romantic
taking.
            Downslope's another whom only death
became, at his world's end, a sailor
struck down in conflict which he did not comprehend,
George Minikin. Margaret Ann walks
inspecting, from one to other.

PEEHI/BEST

Depression, winter of 1930:
He frequented Government House, the Bledisloes
wanting to learn the right way with Maori.
Loneliness grew like rain forest lichens.

From his room at the Turnbull he stared
broodingly at Wadestown high places
as though. Baucke died,
a fortnight after him Pomare in a strange land.
Then Buck, passing through from the Cooks
on his way to Honolulu—Peehi guessed
he wouldn't be seeing Buck again.
Somebody knocked at his door.

Another old man, come to say "The last time
I saw you, you were . . ." lugging weapons, weirdly
kitted out, footslogging, sixty years before
on the track to Manaia, the Armed Constabulary
off to build themselves a fort.
Never again.
Catching a glimpse of him, who would have thought
he was famous? He didn't feel like that,

tired, urgent. He tumbled under a small stroke
not to take seriously. He was sometimes
taken in.
          One year more. When he went
people were upset: by his own wish, he was cremated.
Noone could have the honour of caring.

If you are driving through the Park—
it is his as much as anyone's memorial—
you can afford him a moment's remembering
at Heipipi where two streams still run clean,
joining, headwaters of the Whakatane River.
You may even recall a line he wrote:
'Think not, O Children of the Earth,
our parents' love is dead.'

        was from a German missionary
family
        which came to the Chathams, off
from the Middle Island,
                    which is   off
by (say) 600 miles
                and they were
off the main island where they arrived
at but somehow (for God's sake, can you
imagine how?) he grew into
                love of the classics,
commanded languages.

              He worked
on the North Island, especially the King
Country. Perhaps what he read had
in several languages
                something to do with
his sense of justice and injustice
particularly about the Treaty.

        When he died, he died in Otorohanga
where people who may not know about
Baucke
        try to do something   about
preserving kiwi, which are
        endangered species.

RINAUA/LINDAUER

What palace corridor does she tenant,
what became of, the girl with clematis around
her head
                    admired by Edward Prince of Wales
and given him, eighteen eighty-five?

A long haul
                    from the India and Colonial Exhibition,
from the World Fair at St Louis, nineteen four.
Offers were made
                    along with the grand prize and gold
medal, of the Palace of Art. A long haul
from Vienna
clean out of sight from Pilsen,
    his church images, his Nazarene mentors.
How far
                    between his paintings,
his subjects' world,
                            and his. Ex voto.

In a main street dairy dedicated to rugby
HART is getting a going over.
There's a special on riding boots for pony club
members a couple of shops along,
what else is special one may not hazard.
Why, you ask, did he settle here?
And, settled, stay?

Twice he returned to Europe, briefly.
He travelled the country, yes, but also
sitters came to him. He wasn't a landscape man.

This wasn't (and isn't) in that sense 'landscape'
country. When you think
                            what it was like,
what old photographs tell . . .

    Sheepdogs penned on a utility stare
perplexedly. Mongrel Mob riders passing through
do not look sideways at the black and white
at an intersection, idling.

In the dairy they argue about apartheid,
bringing things down to black and white.

POMARE

Tainui's anchor stone keeps its proper distance
up the road. A local tourist brochure has
things arse about face. Never mind, we can live
with that. At least, they seem able.
This isn't Tainui country. This isn't
what it used to be.

Pomare and Buck were much of an age,
they saw day first in the same place which is not
same. And won't be, day by day.
Motunui stands between them almost halfway,

rigs, gantries, its several shapes
which are of things to come.

Buck remembered Pomare returned from the States,
'top hat, frock coat, and striped trousers that characterized
the profession in those days' . . . 'Dr Pomare and I
      divided
the North Island between us.'
In South Africa lands were being divided between,
barbed, wired. Shadow, and overshadow.
They went their ways.

Like anatomies. Think Big steels diagrammatize
a made-over prospect. Pomare, he's buried with
Sicilian marbles, Sicilian granite.
You'd have thought, they had enough stones of own kind.

TE RANGI HIROA/BUCK

Te Rangi Hiroa is sleeping
at Oroki, outside Urenui.
There he and Pomare were boys.

Offsea winds arrive to make their blades keen;
every so often they need to come, to sharpen.
They rub on the canoe's prow, perhaps
they have questions.

Buck had questions. Wherever he went
he mightn't ask outright—he knew how to behave—
of this one and that one, or of this one and that knew
alright to say directly "Tell me . . . Show me".
Said "Show me how they tie a knot and I'll tell you
something worth knowing about these people."
Looking down the land to Petrocorp,
it makes you wonder, doesn't it?

He went up and down dividing the North Island.
Later, he went up and down in many islands.
Knew this, getting to know that. He liked knowing.
Knowing today, knowing only something about yesterday.
Once he dreamed a long, very detailed, dream
about a marae on Nukuhiva (he wasn't half-Irish for nothing)
where he hadn't been. A voice said
'To ha'afiti ia Te 'Ani Hi'oa. This share for
        Te Rangi Hiroa.'
That was his share. Can we, he wrote, ever
see the throbbing past except in dreams?

So there he is, only ashes, but dreaming in his sleeping.
Catching up with, all that he didn't get to know.
Somebody robbed the gravegoods.

Buck hadn't been to the Marquesas.
All he had were Linton's diagrams. 'I do not wish
to awake, for when I do, I will see but a line drawing
in a book that conjures up a lone terrace overgrown
with exotic weeds, and sad stone walls crumbling to
    decay.'
He did not mean, to refer to Petrocorp.

Think not, O Children of the Earth, our parents' love
    is dead.

NOTES

People have asked about some points of detail, so briefly some answers.

Dreams, Responsibilities. Alessandro Marcello (1684–1750), one of a well-known family of Venetian musicians.

Skateboarding with Lewis Carroll. 'I mark this day with a white stone' is an expression which Carroll uses for what he regards as notable occasions.

Promise. The Prophet here is Te Kooti who is also the Turuki of *Mountain Stop.*

Pivoting. Taratara is the big rocky feature inland from Whangaroa, the road taken is through the Otangaroa Valley, the eventual terminus is Kohukohu.

Legend of Sara's Gully. Sara Milhall is fictitious, and the gully is not Sarah's Gully on the Coromandel coast. The story is worked up from one told me by Michael Neill, of another part of New Zealand.

Movements for Coastal Voices. This takes some liberties with Sir George Grey. The scene is Wenderholm. The visiting professors (German and Celtic) were from Texas. The German quotation is from Goethe. Stefan George's friend was Karl Wolfskehl, and the allusion is to his poem 'The Fig Tree'.

Reading the Maps. Mahimai is John Marmon, also known as Tiaki, the first and most notorious white settler in the Hokianga, who figures in various memoirs including his own. John Rutherford—which is almost certainly not his real name—was the once celebrated tattooed white man whose account of living with Maoris appeared in *The New-Zealanders* (1830). I regard it as the first sustained piece of fiction about this country.

Of Sorts. The sentence 'This world . . .' is from Sir Thomas Browne, *Religio Medici.*

Christ Church Yard, 1984. Reverend Robert Burrows was the first incumbent of Christ Church, Russell. The German is from the Rückert song 'Wenn dein Mütterlein . . .'.